KNOWING JESUS

Peter Rodgers

InterVarsity Press
Downers Grove
Illinois 60515

InterVarsity Press is the book-publishing division of Inter-Varsity Christian Fellowship,
a student movement active on campus at hundreds of universities, colleges and
schools of nursing. For information about local and regional activities,
write IVCF, 233 Langdon St., Madison, WI 53703.

Distributed in Canada through InterVarsity Press, 1875 Leslie St., Unit 10,
Don Mills, Ontario M3B 2M5, Canada.

ISBN 0-87784-383-X

Printed in the United States of America

Library of Congress Cataloging in Publication Data

Rodgers, Peter, 1943-
    Knowing Jesus.

    Bibliography: p.
    1. Jesus Christ–Person and offices.   2. Jesus
Christ–Knowableness.   3.   Christian life–1960-
I. Title.
BT202.R613   1982   232   82-14832
ISBN 0-87784-383-X

15	14	13	12	11	10	9	8	7	6	5	4	3	2	1
92	91	90	89	88	87	86	85	84	83	82				

One
Where Do I Begin?

"I WANT TO KNOW MORE ABOUT JESUS, but where do I begin?"

Have you ever asked this question? This book is written for people who want to know what it means to be a Christian, to know and trust God, and to have a personal relationship with him through Jesus Christ. Some who read it may not even believe in God. Others may know a lot about the Bible and its message, but wonder why it does not seem to relate to their lives. Still others may never have given these things serious thought. In short, this book is meant for any person, believer or unbeliever, informed or uninformed. The only thing it assumes is that its reader is making a serious attempt to ask such questions as these: What is Christianity? Is it true? Is it true for me?

"But where do I begin?" Let us try to answer this question by rephrasing it, "How do I begin?" People are interested in how things are done and how they work. We want to get inside things, to analyze and explore them. We must, however, have the right approach to Jesus; otherwise we will miss the point or make him into something he is not. The right approach in thinking about Jesus is to give him a fair chance. Let him speak for himself. Here are five questions that may guide you and serve as a check list.

Am I Interested?

Many people look at Christianity with little genuine interest. They remain detached from the subject. Among their reasons for thinking about Christianity at all are the following: social—they go to church because it is the thing to do; intellectual—they are curious about theology or need to study religion for a term paper; or antiquarian—they like old things and the church seems like the oldest thing around. The key question is, Do they care what Christianity has to say to them?

If you are not genuinely interested in Christianity as a way of life, you will never know what it is all about. You may study it for years and know lots of details, but to know it from the inside you have to know what it means to you. You must be personally interested. "Seek, and you will find," said Jesus Christ (Mt 7:7). He echoed the words of the Old Testament prophet Jeremiah, through whom the Lord said to Israel, "You will seek me and find me; when you seek me with all your heart" (29:13). Not until you seek God with all your heart will you find him as fully as he can be found.

Am I Honest?

Begin where you are. Only accept what you can honestly believe or understand. Many people find the Christian faith impossible because they think it forces them to begin where they are not and to believe what they cannot. If ours is a fair God, he will not do this to you. Jesus' contemporaries followed him because he met them where they were. He did not say to them, "You have to come up to my level before I will talk with you or care about you." He listened to each person regardless of weakness, doubt, fear or sin. He even ate with the people whom everybody considered to be common sinners (Lk 15:1-2). He spent time with both the influential and ordinary. He did not care how much money a man made or whether he was a prominent citizen. He got alongside people from all walks of life, high and low, rich and poor. As a result, people could be honest when they were around Jesus. He was not impressed with mere externals but with a person's inner qualities.

The story in John 9 of a blind man gives us a good example of an honest man who met Jesus. Jesus came along, found a man blind from birth and gave him his sight. The man believed in Jesus and was made to see by a simple act of obedience. Immediately all the religious leaders of the day tried to find out what had happened. They asked the man questions, some of which he could not fully understand. Faced with questions beyond his grasp, the man replied that he did not know the answers, but "one thing I know, that though I was blind, now I see" (v. 25). He said only what he knew and described only what he had experienced. Because he was honest, however, he came in a short time to believe a great deal. You will be able to do the same if you are honest and admit only what you know to be true. Honesty is risky, though. You may be forced to change your mind about God. You may be challenged by the Word of God to change the way you live.

Am I Humble?

If you find Jesus' claims about his identity to be true, then have the humility to admit it. The only mind that can learn anything new is the humble mind, the mind that says, "There's a lot I don't know. I must be taught." The only heart that can find acceptance with God, according to the teaching of Jesus, is the humble heart. Some people seek God with interest and honesty, yet when they find him they decide that it would be too costly to obey him. Like the rich young man of Matthew 19: 16-22, they find it too hard to obey Jesus because everything else in their lives would have to take a lesser priority to him. The young man did not have the humility to obey, even though he knew that what Jesus taught was true. He went away disappointed.

Without humility of mind, heart and will, you too will be disappointed in your search for God. Consider the following modern parable, reminiscent of that in Luke 18:9-14.

Two students went to their laboratories. One was a brilliant young research fellow and the other a struggling first-year student. It was their habit while waiting for equipment from the stores, or for their apparatus to warm up, to sit and think about life. The

8

research man thought to himself. "I am glad that I am not like some men, or like people of past ages, in bondage to creeds and rules, or even like that student. I have passed my exams. I can beat anyone in an argument and I base my actions on reason alone."

The other did not trust his thoughts very far. He buried his head in his hands and said, "God teach me what life is all about. I am ignorant and confused."

This student learned more than the other, for everyone who is proud of his own intellect will be disillusioned, but the man who is humble enough to seek the truth will find it.[1]

Be humble as you take a serious look at Christianity, recalling the words of President John F. Kennedy, "Humility is never a sign of weakness."

Am I Prayerful?

If God is real and if he is personal, we can talk with him. From the very first you should ask him to help you in your search. You may have to pray like the man who cried to Jesus, "I believe; help my unbelief!" (Mk 9:24). You may feel that you do not know how to pray. You may feel as if you are talking into midair, or that you are just talking to yourself. Many people feel this way when they first start to pray. It may feel awkward, but if God is there and if we can talk with him, we have to begin somewhere. Perhaps you may want to start with a simple honest prayer that goes something like this:

O God, if you exist (and I am not sure if you do) and if you can hear this prayer (and I do not know if you can), I want you to know that I am an honest seeker of the truth. My mind is open; I am willing to believe. I am ready to obey. Teach me the truth. Show me if Jesus is your Son and the Savior of the world. And if you help me to see him, help me also to make the right response to him.[2]

God honors and will answer such interest, honesty and humility.

Am I Informed?

We are thinking and praying about Jesus, so we shall want to know about him. The best way to do this is to consult the Bible. It is *the* primary source: the only Jesus we shall be considering is the Jesus portrayed in the Bible. Christians in every age have trusted the Bible as God's revelation of himself, so let it speak for itself. Listen to the words of Christ; think about the deeds of Christ. Seek to know who he was, and what he said and did. (For a helpful introduction see *Understanding the Bible* by John R. W. Stott, Zondervan.) If he gives a command like "love your neighbor as yourself," try phrasing that command into a prayer such as "Lord, help me to love my neighbor." If he gives a promise like "seek and you shall find," turn it into a prayer such as "Father, help me to find you. You promise that I will." This way of praying biblically has helped many seekers grow into faith.

But can we trust the Bible? Are the Gospels, for instance, reliable records about Jesus Christ? Such questions are common. The Gospel narratives are not precise biographies but "interpretive portraits." Nevertheless, they are as trustworthy as any ancient history. My own technical study of the New Testament has led to an ever-deepening confidence in its reliability, a conviction shared by many engaged in the study of Christian origins. (The best short discussion on the subject is *The New Testament Documents: Are They Reliable?* by F. F. Bruce.)

Try to understand what the Bible says and how it applies to you. That is surely the place to begin, and from there take one step at a time. You must be informed of what the Bible says before deciding whether or not it is true. You have no right to make a final decision about Jesus Christ until you know the facts about him. Then you may disagree with or disbelieve in him—if you can.

"You will find me," is his promise. It is either true or not true. Will you try it and see if the promise is true?

Two
Who
Is
Jesus?

POSE THE QUESTION WHO is Jesus? to ten people selected at random and what would you get? Ten different answers. Though the answers would vary, you can be sure that everyone would say something. I would guess that more has been said, written and thought about Jesus than about any other person in history. Still it is surprising how few people know what the Bible actually teaches about him.

In this chapter we shall look closely at Jesus. We shall examine the plain teaching about him which we find in the New Testament. Most of our information comes from the four Gospels: Matthew, Mark, Luke and John. They give us four different ways of seeing Jesus, but all draw from similar sources such as eyewitness accounts, collections of Jesus' teachings and recollections of his closest followers. These Gospels are not just the ideas of four men about Jesus; they contain information from the first generation of Christian believers.

His Teaching

One of the first things we notice about Jesus is that he spent a lot of time teaching. His favorite method was to use parables. Jesus would tell a simple, human story in order to illustrate some great principle. Thus, when he was criticized by the religious leaders for eating with common sinful people, he answered them not by a direct argument but by telling three parables (the lost sheep, the lost coin and the lost son), thus illustrating the great truth that God values, knows and accepts all kinds of people (Lk 15).

Often he began his parables by saying, "The kingdom of heaven is like . . ." Then he would go on to tell a story or to paint a picture in words that would show that God's ways are surprising. God can do a lot with just a little. Jesus likened the kingdom of heaven to a grain of mustard seed (Mt 13:31-32; 17:20). It is the smallest of seeds when it goes into the ground, but it grows into a great tree. He concluded that a person's faith may be tiny at first, but if it is real it will produce great results. Jesus' teaching was simple and practical; large crowds gathered to hear him.

Jesus did not teach only in parables. To his closest followers he often spoke proverbs and precepts. The Sermon on the Mount is the best and longest example of the direct teaching of Jesus. In this sermon, recounted in Matthew 5:1—7:29, Jesus describes basic principles of godly living. Straightforward statements, such as "Al-

ways treat others as you would like them to treat you"
(7:12 NEB), gave people a clear and memorable idea of
what their lives ought to be like. Whether in parable or
in precept, Jesus' teaching was so clear, so down-to-earth,
that it drew people to him. This is what we shall discover
as we look into the teaching of Jesus for ourselves. It is
practical; it works. Perhaps you will agree with the sol-
diers who came to arrest Jesus. After they heard him
teach they declared, "No man ever spoke like this man!"
(Jn 7:46).

His Conduct

Actions speak louder than words. Did Jesus live his message as well as teach it? Did he actually live up to his own
standard, or was he a hypocrite? Was his the sinless life
he set as a standard for other people?

The Bible writers are of one mind in claiming that
Jesus lived a sinless and perfect life. Whether from his
own lips or from the pens of his followers, the description
of Jesus is the same (Jn 8:29; Heb 4:15). He remained
fully obedient to God throughout his life. Some people
suppose that in order to do this he must have had some
special protection other people do not have. There is no
evidence in the New Testament that this was the case.
Also, the writer of the letter to the Hebrews states in a
candid passage that Jesus was tempted in every way that
we are, yet he did not sin. Moreover, look at the tempta-
tion recorded in Matthew 4 and Luke 4. These were real
temptations: to turn stones into bread instead of feeding
on God's words, to throw himself off the Temple to force
God into making a dramatic rescue, to gain the world's

14

kingdom in exchange for worshiping Satan. Jesus lived a real human life with real struggles and difficulties just like the people of his day, and just like you and me. Again, the best way to see this for yourself is to read the Gospels and ask whether the Jesus we find there was justified in saying that he always did the things that pleased his Father.

If Jesus' conduct was sinless, it was also self-sacrificing. He sacrificed himself to serve others. He got involved with people; he cared about them, great and small. When he recognized injustice in society he spoke out and acted against it, even when such protests endangered his life. When he saw a man who was sick in body or in mind, he reached out in love to heal that man, even when it made him unpopular with some of the leading people. From start to finish, Jesus lived a life of humble, self-giving service. There is no more beautiful and stirring picture than that of Jesus in John 13, stooping like a common slave and washing his disciples' feet. By making it his task at the Last Supper, Jesus dramatized how he would serve them in a far deeper way: his life of service was crowned by his death of sacrifice.

His Claims

Perhaps what's most striking about Jesus, particularly in light of his character and his conduct, are his extraordinary claims. He was always talking about himself; he seemed to be the center of his own message. His conduct was so self-forgetful, yet his claims were so self-centered. This may surprise you at first, but the more you read the Gospels, the more you will see that Jesus, so humble in his treatment of others, made amazing claims about himself.

"Who do men say that I am?" Jesus once asked his followers. They answered that some said he was Elijah or Jeremiah or an Old Testament prophet arisen from the dead; others said he was John the Baptist. But Jesus went on, "But who do you say that I am?" (Mt 16:13-15). Wherever he went, he seemed to be the center of attention. By what he said and by what he did, he forced people to consider him and make a response to him. No man has ever made such claims as Jesus made. We find these claims in all four Gospels, but they are most frequent in John's account. Consider these:

> I am the bread of life; he who comes to me shall not hunger, and he who believes in me shall never thirst. (6:35)

> I am the light of the world; he who follows me will not walk in darkness, but will have the light of life. (8:12)

> I am the door; if any one enters by me, he will be saved, and will go in and out and find pasture. (10:9)

> I am the good shepherd. The good shepherd lays down his life for the sheep. (10:11)

> I am the resurrection and the life; he who believes in me, though he die, yet shall he live, and whoever lives and believes in me shall never die. (11:25-26)

I am the way, and the truth, and the life; no one comes to the Father, but by me. (14:6)

I am the vine, you are the branches. He who abides in me, and I in him, he it is that bears much fruit, for apart from me you can do nothing. (15:5)

Before Abraham was, I am. (8:58)

I am the Son of God. (10:36)

What remarkable things to say! In plain English, Jesus claims to be able to satisfy our deepest hunger and thirst, and to give us direction, security, freedom and fulfillment. He claims to be the only one who can truly lead us because he is the only true and living way to God. He claims to bring us life, both before and after death. He claims to have the very name of God himself. ("I AM" is the name God gave himself in Exodus 3:14 when he commissioned Moses to lead the people of Israel.)

But do the other three Gospels give us essentially the same picture of Jesus? Yes, Jesus is again the center of his own message, although his claims in these Gospels are presented in a slightly different way. Here we find the same self-assertion and the same apparent egocentricity. Several times in John's Gospel Jesus refers to himself as the Son of man. It is his favorite term when speaking of himself, according to Matthew, Mark and Luke as well. *Son of man* may sound strange to our ears. In fact, some people have thought that Jesus used the term to refer to his humanity, just as the *Son of God* refers to his divinity. But this is unlikely.

For any Jew of Jesus' day who knew what we now call the Old Testament, the "son of man" was an important figure. First, the term *son of man* was a Jewish way for a teacher to refer to himself or to make statements of great significance. Second, when Jesus used this name for himself, his listeners would most certainly remember some familiar words about a future king who was "like a son of man" and to whom

> was given dominion and glory and kingdom,
> that all peoples, nations, and languages should serve
> him;
> his dominion is an everlasting dominion,
> which shall not pass away,
> and his kingdom one that shall not be destroyed.
> (Dan 7:14)

Thus to the Jews of Jesus' time, "son of man" was a special name of greatness, a name given to the ruler whom everyone would serve. We must imagine, then, that when the humble carpenter from Nazareth used this name to refer to himself he was saying, "I am this great king whom you read about in Daniel's prophecy."

In fact, everywhere you look in the Gospels, you find the same Jesus. You simply cannot turn a page of the New Testament without stumbling upon some stupendous claim. It may be a direct claim like the "I AM" statements, or a more indirect claim such as a miracle that demonstrated his power over natural forces. Often he did things that only God had the authority to do: for example, he forgave sins (Mk 2:5-12), and he raised a dead man out of his tomb (Jn 11). In calling people to a new life, he did not say, "Come to God" but "Come to me." He did not say, "Follow God" but "Follow me." He certainly was convinced of his own importance.

Many people easily acknowledge Jesus as a great moral teacher, perhaps the greatest teacher. Others find it easy to see Jesus as a great servant, perhaps the greatest of all servants. But when they come face to face with these claims of Jesus, they have great difficulty with them. "He cannot have said these things," they say. And yet he did.

The British scholar and author C. S. Lewis wrote some thoughtful and witty words about this paradox, showing how Jesus was the only great moral teacher in the world's history who also had a lofty view of himself:

> There is no parallel in other religions. If you had gone to Buddha and asked him, "Are you the son of Brahma?" he would have said, "My son, you are still in the vale of illusion." If you had gone to Socrates and asked, "Are you Zeus?" he would have laughed at you. If you had gone to Mohammed and asked, "Are you Allah?" he would first have rent his clothes and then cut your head off. If you had asked Confucius, "Are you Heaven?" I think he probably would have replied, "Remarks which are not in accordance with nature are in bad taste." The idea of a great moral teacher saying what Christ said is out of the question.[3]

What if you had demanded of Jesus, "Tell us if you are the Christ, the Son of God"? He would have answered you as he did the high priest at his trial, "You have said so" (Mt 26:64). What Jesus said about himself and allowed others to say about him was either the most tremendous lie, or it was the truth.

Some people have suggested that the very combination of his lofty claims and his lowly conduct is the strongest argument for his divinity. His earliest followers, however, had yet another reason to say that he was "the image of the invisible God" and that "in him all the fulness of God was pleased to dwell" (Col 1:15, 19). They believed that he had risen from the dead.

His Resurrection

Did Jesus really rise from the dead? The Christian faith stands or falls on this crucial question. If Jesus did not rise from the dead, then in the words of Paul a Christian's trust in God is futile (1 Cor 15:13-19). But if Jesus has been raised from the dead and is still alive today, then we will want to ask, "How can I know him?"

Many people have tried to deny the resurrection, often choosing one of two ways. They have tried to discredit the records, or they have attempted to show that the resurrection itself did not occur. We shall look briefly at each attempt, starting with the records.

Were the stories merely made up by Jesus' followers, or do they report with reasonable accuracy the events of that first Easter morning and the following weeks? All the accounts of the resurrection (and almost all the Gospel material) were probably completed within the lifetimes of those who had witnessed the things being reported. Before the various stories were finally written down as we have them today, they made the rounds in oral and written form of various Christian communities, where eyewitnesses would approve or disapprove of the way the story was being told. This preserved the essential stories and kept falsehoods from creeping in. Some stories, like that of the Emmaus walk in Luke 24:13-35, would appear to have been told to the Gospel writer by the traveling companions themselves.

The final court of appeal is your own reading. Do the records sound faked to you? Do they sound made up? Or do they possess from start to finish what J. B. Phillips, a well-respected Bible translator, calls "the ring of truth"? Can we believe that the crucified Jesus really rose out of the tomb on the third day and is alive today?

This leads us to examine the second area of disbelief, the resurrection itself. Five lines of reasoning will help us think through this question: the disappearance of the body, the reappearance of the Lord, the emergence of the church, the witness of the Scriptures and the presence of the Spirit.

The body of Jesus disappeared. If you had been among those who went to the tomb of Joseph of Arimathea on that first Easter morning, you would not have found the body of Jesus. Why? Five possible explanations have been given. (1) The disciples and friends might have gone to the wrong tomb. We must reject this explanation. Any doubter could have dispelled the rumor of resurrection by simply going to the right tomb! (2) The friends of Jesus stole the body, hid it and said that he rose from the dead. This theory, however, does not explain the certainty and conviction with which Jesus' followers preached and died for him. Also, a Roman guard had been placed at the tomb to prevent just such a theft (Mt 27:62-66).

(3) The enemies of Jesus stole the body, perhaps to prevent his friends from doing so. But think how easy it

would have been for them to produce the body or other evidence of its theft when Peter began to proclaim Jesus' resurrection. They did not because they could not. (4) Jesus never died on the cross, but feigned death and was laid in the tomb from which he escaped after three days. This theory, popularized by Hugh Schonfield in *The Passover Plot,* raises more problems than it solves. Could such a Jesus, marred and weakened by his ordeal, have rolled a large boulder away from the tomb? Could he, in need of food and medical attention, have so soon convinced his followers that he was the Lord of heaven and earth?

No, the easiest and best explanation of the empty tomb is the one which the New Testament gives: (5) The tomb was empty because Jesus had risen. His body rose, not just his spirit. The Jews of Jesus' time considered a person to be a body-spirit unity; therefore, for first-century Judaism, resurrection meant bodily resurrection.

Each of these possibilities was carefully weighed by Frank Morison, a lawyer who set out to prove once and for all that Jesus did *not* rise from the dead. Based on the evidence he uncovered, he became a convinced believer in the risen Christ. You can read about his fascinating search in *Who Moved the Stone?* (InterVarsity Press).

Jesus appeared to his followers.   At the end of each Gospel, in the beginning of the Acts of the Apostles and in 1 Corinthians 15, a number of instances in which Jesus appeared to his friends are recorded. Even the most unbelieving of writers cannot deny the genuineness of these accounts; he or she feels compelled to explain them away. The most striking of these is recorded in 1 Corinthians

15:6, where Paul rehearses for the skeptical Corinthian church what seems to be an authoritative list of resurrection appearances. He says artlessly that Jesus Christ appeared after his resurrection to more than five hundred believers at one time, and that most of them were still alive (twenty years later) to verify the report.

This was no hallucination: visions occur to individuals but not to groups. This was no wishful thinking: none of the followers of Jesus expected him to rise, although he had predicted it. Paul puts his faith on the line and seems to say to the Corinthians who doubted the resurrection, "Hundreds of people saw the risen Lord at one time. That wasn't too long ago, so many of them are still alive and have probably spread out from Jerusalem. At least some of these witnesses live in or near Corinth. Go ask them what they experienced—see if the stories are the same and make up your own mind about the resurrection."

The church began to grow. How can we explain the rapid growth of the Christian movement in the Roman world of the first century, considering the odds against it? Michael Green writes of these early Christians:

> It was a small group of eleven men. . . . They were not distinguished; they were not well-educated; they had no influential backers. In their own nation they were nobodies, and in any case, their own nation was a second-class province on the eastern extremity of the Roman map. If they had stopped to weigh up the probability of succeeding in their mission, even granted their conviction that Jesus was alive and that his Spirit went with them for their task, their hearts must surely have sunk, so heavily were the odds

weighed against them. How could they possibly succeed? And yet they did.[4]

These apostles, it is believed were put to death for Christ. Can we believe it was for a lie they concocted? For a fable, a myth, a groundless hope?

The Scriptures took on new meaning. The Old Testament was the Word of God to the Jews of Jesus' time. They searched these Scriptures to hear of God's promise to them. They found in the Scriptures God's promise of a messiah, an anointed one who would deliver God's people and establish his kingdom. After Jesus' death and resurrection, his followers read the Old Testament in light of these events. Suddenly, obscure passages began to make sense. His death had been foretold in detail:

They have pierced my hands and feet—
I can count all my bones—they stare and gloat
  over me;
they divide my garments among them,
  and for my raiment they cast lots. (Ps 22:16-18)

The significance of his death was foreshadowed:

Surely he has borne our griefs and carried our sorrows;
yet we esteemed him stricken, smitten by God, and
  afflicted.
But he was wounded for our transgressions,
  he was bruised for our iniquities;
upon him was the chastisement that made us whole,
  and with his stripes we are healed.
All we like sheep have gone astray;
  we have turned every one to his own way;
and the LORD has laid on him the iniquity of us all.
  (Is 53:4-6)

24

The followers of Jesus began to see how the Scriptures had predicted "the sufferings of Christ and the subsequent glory" (1 Pet 1:11). I find it hard to understand this radically new understanding of the Scriptures apart from the resurrection. The New Testament in fact indicates that it was the risen Jesus himself who showed the disciples that he was the object of these Old Testament predictions. As he explained the Scriptures to his two friends on the road to Emmaus he asked, "Was it not necessary that the Christ should suffer these things and enter into his glory?" (Lk 24:26).

The Holy Spirit of Christ came to dwell in believers. Countless men and women today know the power and presence of the risen Christ, just as the first apostles did. Through the ages, the power of the risen Christ has changed people's lives; perhaps you have read about them in books such as *Born Again* by Charles Colson, *Run Baby Run* by Nicky Cruz or *The Late Liz* by Gert Behanna. Or perhaps you have seen movies such as *Chariots of Fire* or *The Hiding Place.* This is one of the most convincing forms of evidence for the resurrection. People today know the risen Christ, and their lives are a powerful witness to him.

None of these five lines of reasoning constitutes absolute proof, but they do make a powerful argument, a convincing body of evidence, for the resurrection.

Consider Jesus Christ. Consider his balanced teaching, his humble service to others, his lofty personal claims and his bodily resurrection. Do you see why his first followers said that the carpenter from Nazareth was the Son of God, the very person of God himself in human flesh? Do you see any reason that you cannot say the same?

Three
Why Did Jesus Come?

E VERY CHRISTMAS, PEOPLE all over the world are faced afresh with the question: Why did Jesus come? It is posed by Christmas carols we hear on the radio or a manger scene we see in a shop window. Even after news of war, we hear "Joy to the World" on the radio. We see Christmas shoppers rush by a manger scene with expensive gifts, apparently unconcerned about the world's starving millions, and we are prompted to ask ourselves, What was the meaning of this birth? Why did Jesus come into the world?

Jesus spoke many times about the purpose of his coming. Let us examine carefully five sayings, looking to Jesus himself for an answer to our question.

He Came to Bring Life
Jesus said, "I have come that men may have life, and may have it in all its fullness" (Jn 10:10 NEB). Surely he knew

the human heart when he said this. People in every age have longed to live life to the fullest, to get the most out of life. Even those in the best of circumstances sense that life could be better than it is.

Events like the death of a loved one or the loss of a job bring people face to face with themselves and cause them to ask about the meaning of life. We all want to know what we are living for and what life holds for us. We want our lives to be worthwhile. Yet time and time again we get a strange feeling that we are missing out on the best part of life. We do not want life to slip like water through our fingers before we have had a chance to savor it. Jesus spoke directly to this longing when he said that he came to give us life in all its fullness.

He Came to Call Sinners

The first three Gospels all record that Jesus said, "I came not to call the righteous, but sinners" (Mt 9:13; Mk 2:17; Lk 5:32). He was speaking to the Pharisees, the religious and social leaders of his day. These people prided themselves on being able to keep the law of Moses. They lived up to its demands, or so they thought, and therefore assumed that they were righteous before God. They felt that nothing more was required of them before they could stand in God's presence. In their care to keep themselves pure, these Pharisees refused to associate with the lower classes, whom they called "sinners."

When Jesus came on the scene, he spent his time with common people. When the Pharisees questioned his fraternizing with these sinners, his answer was plain and direct. He said that people who are well do not need a doctor, but people who are sick do. He reminded them that what God wanted from them was not outward piety but inward purity. Of course God expected them to keep from murder, adultery or stealing in the legal and outward sense. He also required, however, that they should not hate, covet or lust within. They may have kept the outward law to the letter, but their inner lives, their hearts, would tell a different story. Because their whole view of righteousness was concerned with their external actions and not with their internal thoughts, they felt that they were righteous in God's sight when in fact they were not. They could not see their need to turn from sin because they could not see themselves as sinners before God. They felt no need to confess their sins to God, to repent and to turn from unrighteousness.

Jesus had harsh words for these Pharisees. He said that as long as they considered themselves righteous, his message could hold nothing for them because he came not to call those who thought they were righteous, but to call those who knew they were sinners. He taught that all people are sinners, whether they recognize it or not. Listen to his frank assessment of the human condition: "From within, out of the heart of man, come evil thoughts, fornication, theft, murder, adultery, coveting, wickedness, deceit, licentiousness, envy, slander, pride, foolishness. All these evil things come from within, and they defile a man" (Mk 7:21-23).

This is an unattractive list. But Jesus spoke realistically. He did not hide the facts or shrink from the truth, however distasteful. As a result, whether we look at the strife of the world or search the depths of our hearts, we know that Jesus' diagnosis of the human disease is correct. Read the list of these sins again. Does it describe you? Oh, you say, I am not a murderer or an adulterer, and I do not steal from my neighbor. But look at the first item on the list: evil thoughts. Do you ever envy? Are you ever proud or foolish? Do you ever have lustful thoughts? Surely if we take an honest look at ourselves, we have to admit that Jesus' analysis is right. We are sinners; in one way or another we have rebelled against God. The Bible writers use a variety of words to describe our sin and its consequences, such as "missing the mark," "disobeying a voice," "failing," "trespassing," "lawbreaking" and "causing discord." Once we admit this honestly, we shall begin to discover that it was for our sake that Jesus came into the world.

He Came to Save the World

Toward the end of his earthly ministry, Jesus said, "I did not come to judge the world but to save the world" (Jn 12:47). This is tremendous news to us who know we are sinners. We know we are guilty before God. We know we cannot stand in God's presence. We know that God cannot blindly overlook our sins, but must punish us.

If he did not do so, God would be contradicting his own holy and perfect character. We rightly expect that when we come face to face with God, we will first of all hear a word of judgment and condemnation. Do we dare expect anything else? The glorious news of the New Testament is that Jesus did not come to judge the people; he came to save them. As we shall see, he accomplished this mission in the most remarkable way.

He Came to Seek the Lost

One day Jesus reached out to a despised tax collector named Zacchaeus. People immediately objected that Jesus had compromised his standards by associating with this sinner. Jesus replied frankly, "The Son of man came to seek and to save the lost" (Lk 19:10). In these words of Jesus is a clear picture of the human condition. Each person is not merely a sinner who needs to be forgiven and cleansed from sin; each is lost and needs to be found. The Bible writers agree: sin has separated us from God. We are lost. The prophet Isaiah put this truth in unforgettable words: "All we like sheep have gone astray; we have turned every one to his own way." We can rejoice that the prophet continues, assuring us that God has taken the initiative to rescue his lost sheep: ". . . and the LORD has laid on him the iniquity of us all" (Is 53:6).

Not only are people sinners; they are lost. Not only does God save us, he takes the initiative in seeking us. These words look forward to the time when God in his love would send his Son Jesus Christ to rescue us and bring us back to himself.

He Came to Give His Life

Perhaps the clearest statement from Jesus' own lips about his purpose in coming is found in Mark 10:45: "For the Son of man also came not to be served but to serve, and to give his life as a ransom for many." These words bring us to the heart and center of Jesus' mission. We have already seen the importance he claims by taking the Old Testament name "son of man" (see pp. 17-18). The prophet Daniel tells us that all people will eventually serve him.

Now Jesus says that he did not come to be served, but to serve. He came to do something for us. He did not come to take something from us, but to give something to us.

Many people are convinced that the Christian gospel calls us to do good things and that these will put us into favor with God. Nothing could be further from the truth. One Christian leader puts it this way: "The only thing that I can contribute to my own salvation is the sin from which I need to be saved." The Bible's message is not about what we can do for God, but about what God has done for us in Jesus Christ. Many people never come to Christian faith because they never understand this simple truth. Jesus came to serve us, and if we are to be Christians, our first duty is not to serve Christ but to be served by Christ. He came to serve us; we must let him if we are to be his followers.

How does he serve us? The last expression of Mark 10:45 makes it crystal clear. He gave his life as a ransom for many. Jesus came to give his life. He came to die for us. As someone once phrased it, "He came not so much to live his life as to give his life." Because he did not have to give his life as a ransom for his own sins (he had none), he could give it to serve others. So he did.

He said that he would give his life as a ransom for many, his death becoming the ransom price which bought back our relationship with God. Sin had become a wedge, separating us from God. We were spiritually dead, unable to save ourselves, so God in his love sent his Son to die instead of us. This is why he cried on the cross, "My God, my God, why have you forsaken me?" On Christ crucified, God was nailing all the sins that people have ever committed. He had to turn his back on Jesus Christ because he was representing sinners before God. Just before he died Jesus said, "It is finished." This is one word in Greek, *tetelestai,* which was often stamped on bills in the ancient world and meant "paid." The death of Christ accomplished all that was necessary for us to stand in God's presence. "It is finished" is the Christian's Emancipation Proclamation.

The New Testament writers echo these words of Jesus again and again. They all return to his "commercial" language to describe what Jesus did for us. Paul says, "You were bought with a price" (1 Cor 6:20). Peter writes, "You were ransomed . . . not with perishable things such as silver or gold, but with the precious blood of Christ, like that of a lamb without blemish or spot" (1 Pet 1:18-19).

In addition to these pictures from the marketplace, two other images describe how we are brought back into a relationship with God. Legal terms show that, although we are guilty sinners before God the Just Judge, Jesus in his death on the cross assumed our blame. Peter says that Christ "died for sins once for all, the righteous for the unrighteous, that he might bring us to God" (1 Pet 3:18). Paul writes confidently, "There is therefore now no condemnation for those who are in Christ Jesus" (Rom 8:1). If we are "in Christ" (Paul's shorthand for "Christian"), we know that now and on the last judgment day we will stand before God "not condemned." Jesus Christ has already taken our condemnation for us.

Another image, reconciliation, can have a powerful effect on people. Because of sin, people are separated from God, actually enemies of God. "In Christ God was reconciling the world to himself" (2 Cor 5:19). Just as a rebellious child may be brought back into fellowship with loving and patient parents, so we in our rebellion have been brought back into fellowship with God by the costly work of Jesus Christ, the only mediator.

This is the heart of the New Testament message: Jesus Christ died instead of us sinners. To know this is to know why Jesus came into the world. To believe and trust in it is to become the rich beneficiary of his costly work. It is to begin living life at its best. As a modern songwriter puts it:

> All my iniquities on him were laid,
> He nailed them all to the tree.
> Jesus the debt of my sin fully paid;
> He paid the ransom for me.

Four

What Does Jesus Offer & Ask?

If I claim to be a gourmet cook, I am in effect offering a sumptuous meal to any who dine at my table. When my friend claims to be a concert pianist, she is promising to share beautiful music with her audience.

Jesus made some remarkable claims that are perhaps the best indicators of what he offers to those who come to know him. Let us look at each of these statements, all recorded in the Gospel of John. Then we will find out what he asks of us in return.

Jesus Offers to Us ...
The bread of life.   "I am the bread of life; he who comes to me shall not hunger, and he who believes in me shall never thirst" (6:35). Bread and water are the basic elements of survival. Jesus, in claiming to be the Bread of Life and to supply living water (7:37), offers us *satisfaction*

of our deepest spiritual hunger and thirst. Read John 4:1-26; it tells the story of the woman at the well and illustrates how Jesus alone can satisfy people who are keenly aware of their spiritual needs.

The light of the world. "I am the light of the world; he who follows me will not walk in darkness, but will have the light of life" (8:12). Many people wander aimlessly, lacking leadership. Jesus promises *direction* to those who follow him, giving point and purpose to their lives. The blind man in John 9 discovered this: Jesus not only restored his sight but also opened his inner eyes.

The door. "I am the door; if any one enters by me, he will be saved, and will go in and out and find pasture" (10:9). Jesus' contemporaries would have pictured a stone sheepfold with an opening for a door. Jesus is claiming to offer the *security* of the fold, the *freedom* to go in and out at the right times, and the *fulfillment* of the pasture. Coming to know Jesus Christ means not the loss but the gain of a real freedom, a real fullness and a new adventure.

The good shepherd. "I am the good shepherd. The good shepherd lays down his life for the sheep" (10:11). In laying down his life for us and suffering in our stead, Jesus secured for us and now offers to us complete *forgiveness.* This is why Peter says, "For Christ also died for sins once for all, the righteous for the unrighteous, that he might bring us to God" (1 Pet 3:18). "There Is a Green Hill Far Away," a hymn by Cecil Frances Alexander, expresses it this way:

There was no other good enough
To pay the price of sin,

He only could unlock the gate
Of heaven, and let us in.

The resurrection and the life. "I am the resurrection and the life; he who believes in me, though he die, yet shall he live, and whoever lives and believes in me shall never die" (11:25-26). Because Jesus rose from the dead, he can boldly offer us a *life* beyond the grave that is far better than life here and now. When the queen of Sheba visited King Solomon in all his splendor, she said to him, "Behold, the half was not told me" (1 Kings 10:7). If we belong to Christ, that is what we will say when we wake up on the other side of death.

The way, the truth and the life. "I am the way, and the truth, and the life; no one comes to the Father, but by me" (14:6). People try to reach God through many avenues—religious ritual, good works, intellectual achievement—but all are dead ends. Because he alone has lived a life fully pleasing to God, he opened to us *the only way to find God.* He also offers us on the way the companionship and guidance of a real friendship.

The vine. "I am the vine, you are the branches. He who abides in me, and I in him, he it is that bears much fruit, for apart from me you can do nothing" (15:5). Just as the vine gives a vital link between the branches and the stem, so Jesus offers himself as the vital link between God and us. To know Jesus Christ is to have *a living relationship with God.* Jesus himself vividly portrayed this when he said: "Behold, I stand at the door and knock; if any one hears my voice and opens the door, I will come in to him and eat with him, and he with me" (Rev 3:20).

Jesus wants to be friends. He wants to come into our

lives and share life with us, like two people sharing in fellowship over a meal. He does this by sending his Holy Spirit into our hearts when we trust him (Jn 14:16-18). Perhaps as you have read these pages, you have heard him knock on the door of your life. Knowing who he is, why he came and what he offers you, will you open the door to him? You may do so, but first consider carefully what Jesus requires of those who follow him.

Jesus Asks Us For...

Jesus himself outlines the attitudes which we must willingly acquire if we are to know him and follow him:

> And he said to all, "If any man would come after me, let him deny himself and take up his cross daily and follow me. For whoever would save his life will lose it; and whoever loses his life for my sake, he will save it. For what does it profit a man if he gains the whole world and loses or forfeits himself? For whoever is ashamed of me and of my words, of him will the Son of man be ashamed when he comes in his glory and the glory of the Father and of the holy angels."
> (Lk 9:23-26)

As we discussed in the previous section, this Son of man is knocking at the door of your life. He will not force his way in; you have to open the door for him. Imagine that the door has not only a handle but also three large bolts which represent our defenses against God. None of us can undo these bolts without God's help, though our desire to do so indicates that the Holy Spirit is already working in our hearts, prompting us to ask Jesus to enter. Let us look at these bolts and see what is required of

37

anyone who wants to be his follower and friend. Each bolt is labeled with the words of Jesus.

A willingness to forsake sin. Jesus said, "If any man would come after me, let him deny himself" (Lk 9:23). The essence of sin is selfishness and self-centeredness, the impulse to say "me first." We make ourselves—our desires, relationships and things—more important than God, even worshiping them in place of God. Anyone who wants to follow Jesus must be willing to turn his or her back on anything that stands between self and God, determined to say no to anything that displeases God. Jesus used the vivid picture of a person taking up a cross. The image reminds us that Jesus was absolutely clear in his commitment to the Father's will, even though it meant going to the cross of Calvary. If we would follow Christ, we must be just as clear in our turning away from sin and our turning toward him.

A willingness to follow Christ daily. We will not lose the salvation and relationship he has won and we have claimed (Jn 10:27-28). Nevertheless, a consequence of trusting Christ is a determination to follow him daily. We must be willing at all times and in all places to acknowledge him as Lord, the real and final authority in our lives. Jesus warns that if we try to hold onto our lives and to be the final authority over them, we will ultimately end up losing them. If we lose our lives for his sake by turning over the management of our lives to him, we will keep our lives. It is hard to say to Jesus Christ, "Okay, you are the boss," but it is essential if we are to enter into a real relationship with him. He will not travel as a passenger; he wants to be in the driver's seat.

A willingness to be found with Jesus Christ.   Jesus said, "Whoever is ashamed of me and of my words, of him will the Son of man be ashamed when he comes..." (Lk 9:26). In cultures like ours where Christian churches have been welcome for centuries, these words seem tame. In many places, however, to be known as a follower of Jesus Christ is to forfeit a college education or even to risk torture. Though the pressures to deny our allegiance are more subtle in materialistic Western society, to be known as Christ's person is looked upon with increasing ridicule. In years to come it will likely become harder to stand up and be counted for Jesus Christ.

Christians have at times gone out of their way to declare their allegiance without having won the right to be heard or considered in the context in which they are speaking. Jesus does not call for zeal without wisdom. But when we are called to give an account of our relationship with Jesus Christ, we should not shrink from it if we mean to be his disciples. We must be unashamed to be found with him.

The Step of Faith

A willingness to forsake sin, to follow Jesus Christ daily and to be found with him—this is what Jesus requires of those who would follow him. Perhaps you think that it is too much to ask. You may feel that there are old habits, displeasing to God, that will be hard to give up. You may feel that there are aspects of your life, especially your relationships, where you will want to remain in control. You may feel that ridicule from others when they learn that you have begun following Jesus Christ will be more than you can bear. Do count the cost, but as you do, remember what this friendship has cost Jesus Christ. He who was willing to go to the cross for you, to "become sin" for you (2 Cor 5:21), to suffer the agony of separation from God for you, is the one who is knocking on your door and seeking your friendship.

Twenty-five years ago I sensed that Jesus was knocking on the door of my life. I knew I was a sinner, a rebel against God, and I wanted to find forgiveness and the way back to him. Then I heard the words of Jesus: "I am the way, and the truth, and the life; no one comes to the Father, but by me" (Jn 14:6). I invited him into my life and we began a new relationship.

If you have felt that Jesus Christ has been knocking at your door (maybe he has been doing so for a long time and you are finally beginning to hear him), and if you are willing to undo the three "bolts" on your life, then you are ready to invite him into your life and begin this new relationship, which is life at its best. As you sit or kneel (the latter expresses vividly your humiliation before God), pray to Jesus Christ in these or similar words:

Lord Jesus, I sense that you are standing on the outside of my life and want to come in. I admit that I am a sinner and have rebelled against you. I believe that you love me and that you died on the cross to gain forgiveness for my sins and a new relationship with God. I have counted the cost and am prepared to forsake sin, to follow you daily as Lord and to be known as your follower. Come in, Lord Jesus, and begin with me this new relationship, this life at its best. Amen.

Five
What Next?

YOU HAVE BEGUN A NEW LIFE: you have started a relationship with Jesus Christ. You have confessed your sin and rebellion to him. You have claimed his death on the cross as full and complete forgiveness and cleansing. By faith you have received him into your life. His Holy Spirit now dwells within you. Where do you go from here?

Getting to Know God
The Lord who made the heavens and the earth does not leave you to grope your way through a relationship with him. He has provided two main ways to get your friendship started.

Trusting his Word. The Bible is God's Word to us. Through it he speaks in rich and varied ways. The more you read the Bible, the closer you will grow to Jesus Christ because he is the center of its message. God's teaching and guidance through Scripture will be specific. You will find that the God who inspired each of the biblical writers penetratingly understands your own life. As you read, ask yourself, "Is there a lesson to be learned? An example to follow? A warning to heed? A command to obey?" Begin with one of the Gospels, aided by the books listed in "For Further Reading."

Enjoying his friendship. Just as Bible reading allows God to talk to us, prayer enables us to talk with God. Neither side of the conversation should be neglected. You may be self-conscious, or find it difficult to express yourself at first. Just imagine yourself in God's presence. Picture him as he is revealed in Jesus Christ of the Gospels. Many people have found the following four-step pattern of prayer useful:

Adoration. Spend some time worshiping and adoring the Lord who made you, redeemed you and befriended you. Do not hurry through your time of praise: enjoy God's presence. Do not worry about times of silence: they allow you to draw close to God and him to draw close to you. The Psalms are very helpful, especially the last five, which begin, "Praise the LORD . . ."

Confession. The closer you come to God, the more aware you will be of your own sin. Although the price of sin has been paid and the penalty of sin cancelled, you will still sin as a Christian. You will be tempted and will yield during the rest of your life. Only in the life to come will we be fully free from the presence of sin in our lives. When we do sin, we should confess it right away. I find 1 John 1:9 deeply meaningful and encourage you to memorize it: "If we confess our sins, he is faithful and just, and will forgive our sins and cleanse us from all unrighteousness."

Thanksgiving. Thank God for your life and your new life in him. Thank him also for what he has given you. The apostle Paul urged the Thessalonians, "Thank God in all circumstances." Yes, this includes thankfulness to God for his care during disappointments and hardships as well as for joys and privileges. A thankful heart is the clearest sign of growth in the Christian life.

Supplication. Bring your needs to your heavenly Father. If he cares enough about you to send his Son for you and to seek friendship with you, then you can rest assured that he hears your prayers and will answer them. Ask him first for others and then for yourself. Do not be afraid to bring things before him; nothing is too great for his power, and nothing too small for his care and concern. You may find it helpful to make lists of people or things to pray for. Discipline is needed to keep up a life of prayer, but a Christian can do no greater work.

This fourfold pattern of prayer—adoration, confession, thanksgiving and supplication (easily remembered because the first letters of each taken together spell ACTS)—will be helpful to you, especially as you begin your walk with God.

Getting to Know God's People
Your heavenly Father would like you to meet some people—his people. No Christian is an only child, for we have countless brothers and sisters bonded into a family through the Son of God. Let's get acquainted.

Meeting his people. Friendship with Jesus Christ means

friendship with others who know him. Such fellowship should include meeting on a regular basis with approximately six to ten people who study the Bible and pray together. You will be helped by their experience in the Christian life, and they will be encouraged by the freshness of your new-found faith in Christ.

Joining his family. Join a local church if you are not already a member of one. Denomination is not the most important issue because different worship styles suit different people. The key factor is that biblical belief and biblical preaching must be central to the life of the church. Make sure the pastor has genuine confidence in the reliability, trustworthiness and authority of Scripture, and that pastor and people have a desire to be faithful in word and deed to Jesus Christ. Such churches can be found in virtually every Christian denomination.

Sharing his riches. Giving is the essence of the Christian life. We are Christians only because "God so loved the world that he gave . . ." (Jn 3:16). If we are growing as Christians we too will begin to serve others in Christ's name. This service may take many different forms, such as helping needy people or contributing money to missions. As you grow, you will begin to discover the truth of Jesus' words: "The measure you give will be the measure you get back" (Mt 7:2; Mk 4:24; Lk 6:38). That truth will also become real to you as you share with others that the friendship with Jesus Christ which is yours can be theirs. To me, nothing is more thrilling than to be used by God to introduce others to him.

You may be asking, "What if I cannot keep it up? What if I fail in my Christian walk?" When you fall (and

44

you will), Christ can pick you up and offer forgiveness. The stability of your Christian life does not depend primarily on the fact that you are holding on to Christ. Christ is holding on to *you,* and he has promised that he will not fail you: "I will never fail you nor forsake you" (Heb 13:5). "I am with you always, to the close of the age" (Mt 28:20).

Notes

[1]Denis Osborne, *The Andromedans & Other Parables of Science and Faith* (Downers Grove, Ill.: InterVarsity Press, 1978), p. 63.

[2]Adapted from John R. W. Stott, *Basic Christianity,* 2nd ed. (Downers Grove, Ill.: InterVarsity Press, 1971), p. 19.

[3]C. S. Lewis, *God in the Dock* (Grand Rapids, Mich.: Eerdmans, 1970), pp. 157-58.

[4]Michael Green, *Evangelism in the Early Church* (Grand Rapids, Mich.: Eerdmans, 1970), p. 13.

For Further Reading

Basic Christianity
John R. W. Stott presents a clear statement of the fundamental content of Christianity and urges the non-Christian to consider the claims of Christ. *(IVP, paper)*

Beginning with God
James W. Sire gives a basic introduction to the Christian faith, covering the topics of creation, the Fall, redemption, new life in Christ and glorification. *(IVP, paper)*

The Day Death Died
Michael Green weighs the evidence for and against Jesus' resurrection and urges readers to carefully consider his findings. *(IVP, paper)*

The Fight
John White looks at the basic areas of the Christian life—prayer, Bible study, evangelism, faith, fellowship, work and guidance; in this very personal book he offers refreshing insights into the struggles and joys of life in Christ. *(IVP, paper)*

Food for Life
Peter Lee, Greg Scharf and Robert Willcox introduce beginners to increasingly advanced Bible study skills through word, book, character and theme studies. *(IVP, paper)*

Mere Christianity
C. S. Lewis spells out the essentials of Christian belief and practice in this classic which combines "The Case for Christianity," "Christian Behaviour" and "Beyond Personality." *(Macmillan, paper)*

Ring of Truth
J. B. Phillips, a translator, explains why he is convinced that the New Testament is both reliable and true. *(Shaw, paper)*